Simple Silliness
And
Serious Serendipities

A Series
By

pat hopper berney

Simple Silliness and Serious Serendipities

ISBN: 978-0-578-80428-6

DEDICATION

This silly little work of words is dedicated to all my family and friends who inspire me in every way, especially to my brother Don and sister Sandy. I love you all. You are my world and heart.

WARNING—Be Not Offended!

Grammar, Spelling,

Punctuations and such

May be lacking as you

will see—

But the Content of Course—

Not crossing each 'T'

Is what I wished for you—

from me.

TABLE OF CONTENTS

Page

All Scattered About—As You Will See

Chapter One

Families and Friends If You Please

"Big Ducky" Was Her Name

My Great Gramma was so special
"Big Ducky" was her name—
If her grandkids called her anything else
 It'd just wouldn't be the same

ODE TO DONNA

What was important
When I was 10
Going to school
And having a friend

Playing jump rope
And tetherball
And having you Donna
To share it all

As I grew older
11 or so—
I needed a friend
If I felt low

At 12 and 13
I changed a lot
And I needed a friend
So we could shop

Then 14 thru 16
Almost grown by then
For just about everything
I needed a friend

Overnight sleep overs
Up til three
High school activities
You and me—

You were that Friend
You knew me the Best
Through giggles and tears
And all the rest—

What's still important
Way past 10
Is never forgetting
My special Friend

GRANDPARENTS BIRTH ANNOUNCEMENT

G is for the Gifts your children give you

R is that they really are such dears;

A your lucky—you can Always share them

N give in—never let them start the tears;

D is for the many Dolls you buy them

P for games you were too old to play,

A for all the cleaning you had after

R the wreck they left your house today.

E for Every kiss that they will give you

N for every nice thing they will say,

T for all the other Things not mentioned

S for all the Smiles they bring your way.

Put this poem together—

You'll read GRANDPARENTS

A role that really suits you to a T

And so with all our love

We want to tell you

That's again what you're about to be!!

OUCH!
Sprained Ankle—Get Well Soon

Thank you for your note of concern
It really helped a lot...
I'm trying hard to watch my feet
They're the only ones I've got!

I'll do my best to stay aground
That might be hard...you see
Again I feel like flying high
Look up...you might see me!

I wish for you the greatest day
May all your dreams come true
If not today...tomorrow I say
May be the day for you!

Funny Pillows

Last night around...oh...9 o'clock
The UPS came calling...
I wasn't in my jammies...
Now that could be appalling!

A package with my name He left
I thought twas Christmastime...
I quickly opened it and saw
Was Twas from a friend of mine.

The card you sent was very sweet
The message very kind...
But it didn't compare
With what I found
I thought I'd lose my mind.

I laughed so hard at these new pals
They're two of a kind for sure...
If I was sad...I have to say...
That they're indeed the cure!

So thank you very very much
You hit my funny bone...
No matter what life-tune is played...
They provide a Happy Tone!

Confucius...Confusion, Concussion, Contusion...
Answers to a Friend

My Goodness...You are fast
I see you've responded to all my Thoughts...
Now I must put my Thinking Cap on...
For you've said Lots and Lots...

A Partridge in a Pear Tree
A Cartridge I will ne'er see
Perched upon a Carefree
Computer Printer Box!!

Trouble is your Middle Name
Your Wildness maybe we should tame
A Counselor might well feel the same...
Perhaps it's time for talks!

All Office Machines are out of Style
I guess that I would walk a Mile
To not buy Ink, or use a File
But just eat Bagels, Cream and Lox!

Seasons they just come and go
It's just our lot in life and soooo
Somethings are just not ours to know
Like...Why do we get Chickenpox?

To My Insomniac Friend

I hate it when by 4 a.m.
I haven't slept a wink...
I've tossed and turned and nary...
Have I entertained a Blink!

I may be older...that's so true
But I really need my sleep...
For I'm no good without it
And I turn into a Creep!

I know just what you're saying
It's very lonely sitting there...
Computer Spam or Reruns...
Either one just makes you stare!

It's usually cold and irritating...
The clocks all tick away...
Take your pick...choose your time
It's all different...what they say!

The times are different that is true
And they play a different Tune...
Look out the window...it won't lie
You STILL can SEE the MOON!

Now you say that you keep Hours
That are questionable too...
I'm wondering if that Man in the Moon
Quite possibly is YOU?

The Yellow Tin

There upon the Highest Shelf
In my Pantry I did find...
A yellowed tin for Recipes
Jogging Memories of Mine...

My Mother used it often
Adding cuttings from her readings
Chocked full of all those goodies
That she made us for our "eating"

Swiss steak with smothered onions
Spareribs with apple sauce...
A savory menu of wholesome foods
An eye for Thrift and Cost.

Lemon Meringue and Divinity
Mouthwatering Pumpkin Pie
Sloppy Joes and Tacos
And Corned Beef piled on Rye.

The list goes on, I feel a tear
I miss those special meals...
It's not the food that means so much
Just how the loss now feels...

It didn't matter what she made
Just the fact that she was there
Not only feeding bodies
But nurturing, with love and care.
I'm sorry I don't have a box
In which recipes abound...
To leave my Children memories
If one day my box were found.

Dear Pen Pal

Dear Pen Pal,
Thank you so much for your words
They mean a lot you see...
You really make me want to write
So this is for you from me!

I think a pen pal is a wonderful gift
Especially one as creative as you...
I find I'm impressed...to do my best
And dig deep for ideas most new!

I need inspiration...no hesitation
And you encourage that in me...
So thank you my friend...that ear that you lend...
Helps me to be all I can be...

Poems with Friends

Dear Beggin' for Attention
I guess I need to mention
I enjoy your Poems...
Every single one!

I know that time just screams by
I meant to write...
But Oh My
I'm here and I'll continue till I'm done!

There are sooo many things to say
I'm thinking it could take all day
Addressing just the stars
And moon and sun!

I think I'll take another route
And talk about the River Newt
I've heard that he can be a lot of fun...

The only problem is you see...
I made him up...oh silly me
And now my Friend...
I really have to run!

For I have hit that Writer's Block

And I can hear the ticking clock...

And I find NOTHING else to rhyme with Run

Band of Pink

And old cigar...with band of pink
With words..."I Am a Dad"
Made me warm and fuzzy
Knowing I'd made them very glad!

I quickly placed it all inside
Upon the shelf it went...
I never touched it after that
But, oh how much it meant!

Now I am myself...a parent
With a Hat box of my own
Upon a shelf, and dusty
Containing the precious things I won...

So if you...my children...have conspired
To sneak a peek or two...
I hope you felt warm fuzzies
Knowing Of our love for you.

Families
ARE FOREVER

Families are forever
This I know is true
I can't imagine living
Without anyone of you

There's Dad the Family Patriarch
And Mom his second mate
One without the other
Would have been an awful Fate

In our Family there is Sugar
And definitely Spice
We refer to them as Karen and Cheryl
They're everything that's nice

Snips and Snails and Puppy Dog Tails
That's Chip and Scott and Mike
Accompanied by army men
Skateboards, Scooters and Bikes

We've been a Happy Family
Thru out these many years
We have always clung together
Thru lots of smiles and tears

Families are Forever
This indeed has been our vision
I think we managed very well—
This Berney Family Tradition—

Genealogy

Irene Charity Holsapple
Was born to Vessie and Stoie
Also Ruth Elaine Holsapple another girl
And Donald Elliot a boy

Young Harold Stevens Hopper
Was born to Iva and Frank
He was the only child they had
So he held an impressive "Rank"

Now Irene Charity Holsapple
Became Irene Charity Holsapple Hopper
She met and married Harold Stevens you see
So their lives started out quite proper

In time they had a daughter
Patricia Ann Hopper by name
And like most new parents will attest to
Their lives never were quite the same

Paul Edwin Berney was born
To Helen and Marvel you see
And with his sister Shirley Ann
Made up their swell Family

Patricia Ann met Paul Edwin
Becoming Patricia Ann Hopper Berney
They married and 5 children came
Thus begat the Berney Tree

Karen and Cheryl their daughters
Were joined by Chip, Scott and Mike
Together they lived happily
Mom, Dad, Sisters, Brothers alike

Soul Mates

Paul and I were reminiscing about our respective young childhood years. (It's an age thing) and how both of us were stars in our minds! He never really wanted to play with his army men with anyone else—because he was the Leader and knew just where he wanted the soldiers to go and what to say. His sister Shirley refused to play with him by age 4, because she was a star in her own mind as a swimmer and diver. This is just one example. Now, Little Patty on the other hand was the Director, Producer, Choreographer and of course the Star of her own productions—not to forget Singer-Songwriter. She had no siblings yet, but when they came along she became their Manager/Agent. Gramma Hopper loved all the drama 'cause Patty was a star in her own mind as well. It's amazing that Mr. "I am the World Leader" and Miss "Roll Out the Red Carpet" have made any connections at all—these 65 years. --PB

To Paul

Being someone's First Love Is great—
Being their last
Is perfect
Happy Anniversary!

Chapter Two

Memories Brought To Mind

Bella the 4 Pound Yorkie

When you're close to the ground
There's more dirt to be found
That's one reason
I'd like to be taller

I get grass in my face
I don't like the taste
And it's sure to get stuck
In my collar.

The bugs that I meet
And greet on the street
Are bigger than I ever knew

They stand and they stare
Then crawl up my hair
And my nose is their main Waterloo.

Oh let it not rain
For that is a pain
The puddles are too deep to cross

I'm up to my knees
It's cold if you please—
And I exit a mass in green moss.

When the dinner bell rings
And my hungry heart sings
I'm faced with a kibble this BIG!

Don't they know t'would be nice
If they made it like rice!
What do they think?—I'm a pig?

I find it most humbling
When faced with such mumbling
"Oh look, what a silly small thing."

I can bite with the best
I can fight with the rest
I'm small with the heart of a king.

Childhood Games

Jumping Rope and Hopscotch
Pick-Up-Sticks and Jacks
Reading Books and Kick the Ball
Are simply Childhood Facts

Ode to Bella

If there were nothing
In the world to do
You could indulge
In a Dream or Two...

There's nothing better
To boost your Spirit
You can do anything...
And never Fear It!

In your case, for example,
A Star you can be...
You can accomplish it all...
Just Dream, and you'll see.

You want admiration,
Attention and such?
You can have it All...
No matter how much!

One Blue Ribbon—
Or One every Year
I think you will earn one,
Each time you appear...

Just dream up the lights,
Fancy meals, Limos too...
Little K-9s fawning
All over you...
The Pick of the Litter...
The Best in Show
You're the BEST DREAMER
That I'll ever know!

Bella the Brave

When Big Dogs surround me
Or cats come around me,
I gather myself to great heights.

I think they're aware,
And they wouldn't dare
To challenge this "tiger" to fight.

When evening is nigh
And I heave a big sigh,
And look for a place for my nap,

I'm happy I'm small
And not at all tall
Cuz I fit
In my best friend's lap.

My legs are not hanging,
My ears are not banging,
The edge of the sofa or chair,

I'm curled up in a ball
(Cuz I'm not at all tall)
And my master is happy I'm there.

All Before Noon

Memories of a Fourth Grader—First Day—new school—morning recess—girls jumping rope— good news—"Do you want to play?"—Rules—Jump in on your boyfriend's initials—first name and last name—bad news—10 years old—no boyfriend—no life!—Pretend—Randomly pick 2 initials—yea for the new kid—oh no, picked initials of most popular boy in 5th grade—bad, bad news—teasing and humiliation—memories of a fourth grader first day—new school—lunch!— broken thermos. I've learned fourth grade is hard—opt for kickball and eat in the cafeteria.

Summertime Dreams

Vacation time is over
And now I'm home to stay...
I brought my suitcase filled
With sand so I can dig and play!

I tried to pack the ocean
And a crab caught in a net
But the crab ran off and left me
And water leaking, left me wet!

But the sand and I will have great fun
Grand castles will be mine...
Vacation dreams will still abound
And thoughts of summertime.

Saddle Sores

They said I was cute
In my Jodhpurs and Boots...
A mere lassie
Of seven or eight...

Blond curls peeking out
'Neath a had of black felt
Not aware of eminent Fate...

Astride my Black Steed
Smartly awaiting my turn
To enter the large Riding Ring...

I was thrown most hard
Thru a door in a stall
Such a Shock...to a poor little Thing!

I landed on straw
'Neath the legs of a Mare...
Scaring us both...I must say...

She struggled...me too
'Twas such a small space
To get out of each other's way!

I was placed immediately
Right back up on that Beast
Performance expected of course...

True to the Form
The Show did go on
But I really hated that Horse!

I continued to ride
Both English and Western
But my heart wasn't really in it.

As soon as my Jodhpurs
And Boots grew too small...
There was NO buying new ones to fit!

That is my story
Of Horses and Dreams...
Of International Riding Rings

The Dreams of adults
Not a child, of course
So I went on to dreaming MY dreams!

Music to My Ears—Surely Show My Years

You wonder what happened to Elvis
And Frankie, Sammy and Dean...
They haven't gone far...as you will see...
Just turn on your record machine!

Tis said one can't live in the past
But...with that I cannot agree
The music I carry within my soul...
Comes forth when I push "Memory"

Peggy Lee, Rosie and Jo...
It's easy to miss them all...
But ballads or blues...they're yours you see...
By just pointing and clicking "Recall"

I pine for all the good tunes...
It's hard to find them somehow...
But once in a while...
My senses are rocked
And I think "Baby Take a Bow"

And those who make "Good Music"...
Deserve our accolades...
In that short moment we may find...
"Bad Music" simply fades!

So "Keep the Faith" I say
Just Hum or Sing along...
Cuz all those tunes we carry
Have become our "Personal Song"

And maybe we have had a hand
In creating more than noise...
Our Rhythmic meters made our Drums
Much more than "Children's Toys"

Yes life's a song...If sung just right
Let's hope our "Notes" are clear...
So that the Songs we leave behind...
Say..."We Sang Our Best While Here."

Longing To Find Your Memories

Yes it's nice to have those memories
Of a childhood that is past...
But good or bad I think it's true
There are only some that last...

I sometimes often wonder
If the memories that I hold...
Are true...or just imaginings
Of things that I've been told.

We all remember in different ways
Events that come our way...
Are they just wishful thinking...?
Or things that others say?

So what...you never found a box
Upon that shelf so high...
It doesn't mean "You never were"
You're here to say "It's I"

You're "box" was meant for other things
More important...that's a fact...
What's more precious than this piece of pulp?
A boy's shoe...to keep intact?

Now that's a noble calling
And one I've heard before...
A lowly piece of cardboard box
Designed for something more.

Baby books and cameras
Important...they can be...
But they can't replace your baby face
In your families memory.

It sounds like you are lacking
In your early childhood years
And you probably felt much sadness,
And shed a lot of tears...

But look at how you've turned out
In spite of all your trials
What would your life consist of...
If you hadn't walked those miles?

You have an appreciation...
For all you have...I know...
And for those that did the best they could...
Consider them..."Your Box and Bow"

Memories

Memory is an elusive thing
It comes and goes at will...
When I remember ANYTHING
I find it quite a thrill...

Like...what I did two hours ago
Hmmm...Let me think on that...
I believe I turned the TV on...
And simply turned and sat!

I hate to worry about my mind
I can't afford its loss
Too many other things are gone
I am forced to pay the cost!

I've reached the age of Middleness
In fact I think its past
The mold of Elder I'm afraid
In some minds has been cast.

Designers make their clothes you see
For mostly the "Young Tart"
They don't wear well...even if...
You're "dyed" and "Young at Heart"

The Hairdressers of America
Loooove the svelte and fair...
But gals, my age are subject
To Blue dye and pin-curled hair!

Shoes??? Now that's another matter
Cute shoes for my age are rare
However...I find it easy you see
To find the "Orthopedic Pair"

Whimsical Dolls

Just a note to tell you
You're my Hero...yessiree
I've been "Whimsied" and enchanted...
Your Kids have smitten me!

I now have five... (I went for one)
It's impossible to choose...
So now we are surrounded
And to me...that's the greatest news!

There's Big Betty and her BIG FEEEET
The Carrot bearing Bunny
We can't forget the Olde Goat...
To me He is most funny...

Next we have the Little Girl
Astride her Racing Rabbit...
Another girl with striped socks
(This can become a Habit)

Oh...I'm not done...you can be sure
An order I'll soon place...
Cuz Dottie Lue is calling me...
I can't forget her face!

The kids are sitting on my table
In a Goat Cart full of Hay
A Wooden Goat is pulling them
Along their merry way.

Pumpkins, gourds and autumn leaves
This Season's decoration...
Serve them well till Christmas comes
And a brand new Presentation!

I think I have to get a Life...
I love to play...you see
So Thanks again...Your Gift inspires
That Little Girl in Me...

Road Trip Music

I headed up North
For a breath of fresh air
The sunroof was open...
The wind blew my hair

I listened to Barry
I like Manilow
I also like Frank
And songs from Cheryl Crow

I sang with Neil Diamond
With Willy I crooned
Oh yes...Andy Williams
Sang Blue Moon

Eric Clapton's the best
When he plays the blues
And Huey Lewis and I
Sang with the News

I rocked with Ozzy...
Smash Mouth too
And The Beach Boys and I
Surfed the Blue

We did California Dreamin'
Little Surfer Girl too
The Big Bopper and I...
Did...Doo Wop Dee Doo

It was quite a trip
I had up the Coast
But the singing of course
That's what I loved the most!

So here's my advice...
Just have a BALL...
SING, CROON and SCAT
Forget Geritol!

The Hat Box

There once was a hat box
High on the shelf... I saw it there you see
I always wondered what it held...
For it didn't belong to me.

I noticed it first when I was five...
On tiptoe I saw the bow...
But my legs were short, my arms were too
So I had to wait and GROW.

When I was ten, I saw it again
And wondered at the dust...
I thought it odd it had not moved,
And looked at it with lust.

What did it hold? My thoughts ran wild
What treasures could it bare?
I got a stool...turned on the light
And finally climbed up there!

Was there gold or silver in it?
Maybe jewels, like Pirates had?
Was it something of my Mother's?
Or, trinkets of my Dad?

When at last I finally reached it
And I took it off the shelf...
It slipped and fell and opened and...
I really scared myself!

There inside, and spilling out
Were Memories of Me!
Pictures and a Baby Book...
My curl, when I was three.

My first tooth that the Fairy left
My first word and my shoes...
The announcement of my birth was there
Within the Local News.

Saturday Night Movies

So now it's Movies?
What to do...
Do you serve cokes?
And popcorn too?

I'll have to think a bit on this
I've Hero's Big and Small...
There's Gene 'n Roy...there not tall
And JOHN...not short at all!

Patrick Swayze...danced it up
Gene Kelly and Astaire
When he and Ginger Roger danced...
They were the perfect pair.

Then remember Esther Williams
That gal could really swim...
She married that guy Lamas...
Hummmm...I remember him!

Doris Day...a favorite
So Perky and so Cute
Peter Lawford...Ocean's Eleven...
Did he ever get the loot?

Cary Grant made me weep...
And Affair to Remember...Sob
Walter Matthau...opposite Lemmon
Remember? He played the slob.

Rock Hudson...Liz...and Jimmy Dean
All GIANT stars were they...
Clark Gable threw old Scarlett out...
He really made her pay...

I could go on and on and on...
But it's time to go to bed...
Instead of talking Movie talk
I'll Movie dream instead.

God Bless America

Lately I have been thinking of things patriotic—like—in grade school we said the "Pledge of Allegiance" and sang "God Bless America". George Washington proudly looked down at this freshly scrubbed, untainted by the world, group of "Proud To Be American" children. We were taught that we were blessed to live in this free country, and with this came responsibilities—like —during the 2nd World War—I was called into the principal's office and given a loving lesson on why we don't waste paper. We were taught there were children like us, but less fortunate and learned to have empathy and concern for them. We can only hope that the lessons we learned, we have passed down to our children, so that this great country will be preserved in spite of a millions things that seem to be working against it.

Chapter Three

Angel Wings of The Heavenly Kind

Angel Unaware

When I was Small, I had a Friend
That only I could see...
Her name was Light and I'm convinced
She came and stayed with me.

One time my Grampa passed too close
On stairs that we were sharing...
He stepped on Light...the space was tight...
I was crushed at his grave Erring

I know He felt most badly
And I was very sad
For Light was very dear to me
The best friend that I had...

I've often wondered thru the years
Just why I called her Light...
Was she an Angel sent to me?
To help guide me do the right?

Tho I don't see her anymore
As I did when I was new...
New to this Earth from a Loftier Sphere
I know she has work to do...
For she has never left me
Alone to fight the fight
Her Spirit's always close to me
My Friend, My Angel, Light.

Zig Zag Papers

I told you about Grampa
Who stepped on Light one day?
Well here's another memory
Please listen, as I say...

My Grampa smoked tobacco...
Prince Albert in a can...
He rolled it in small papers
'Tween the fingers on his hand...

Now after he would do this
He would extend to me
The newly rolled up cigarette
AND I WOULD LICK IT closed...you see.

Then he would twist the very ends
First one and then the other...
He'd light it up and take a puff...
I'd hold my nose...or smother!

I hold most dear this Memory
I loved my Grampa so
So special was this time we shared
Only He and I could know.

This event was made more special
Cuz we would sit on the old bus bench
On the Corner in the town he lived
In the Sunshine near a fence.

I'd swing my legs...they didn't reach
And wait to see the "Prince"...
Give Grampa Zig-Zag Papers
I've not forgotten...since!

Over The Rainbow Bridge

Last night I took Bella
My sweet little friend
To the Doctor and held her
As she met her end.

She had a bad day
And her eyes pled with me
To help her in some way...
And I did, so you see.

Today is a hard one
But for her, she is free
I pray I did the right thing
For her......not for me........

Table Manners

Don't talk with your mouth full
Close your lips when you chew
Say Yes Please—No Thank You
May I Be Excused—when you are through

Animal Farm

Sitting in a barnyard
With chicken and a cow
Billy goats and piglets too
Is quite the cat's meow!

I Say You Say

On the West Coast
We call it Chowder
On the East Coast
Chowdah is its name
Whatever you choose to call it
It definitely tastes the same

Tattooed You

One tattoo—2 tattoo—3 tattoo 4
It seems like if you get one—
You're destined to get more
I eye the tattoo needle
With fear and yes—suspicion
Thus prompting me to certify
Tattoos?——not my decision

Security

I believe in Heavenly Father
And in Jesus Christ his Son
I Know I am his Daughter
And I know from whence I've come.

I Know where I'll am going
And I know why I am here
I know that I can weather all
If I just keep Him near.

So that is all...there's nothing more
Just strive to stay on Course...
Family, Friends, good works and Love
This is my Driving Force.

Message From Mom

'Twas a warm October Day
When she quietly passed away
She was 82 and now
Her time had come.

Her children gathered round
And no one made a sound
In grief it seemed that
They had been struck dumb.

'Twas a cool November Day
Thanksgiving dinner cooked her way—
Was shared by all—
Whom she had loved the best

Without her loving hand
Would the dinner seem as grand?
Could tradition without her pass the test?

'Twas a cold December Day
As if in a dream—
She came to say
Loving words that only a Mother could

"I'm Happy and I'm fine"
Her spirit spoke to mine
"And the dinner you girls made—
Looked real good"

Oh the months how they do fly
But I know she was near by
And her words still bring me comfort
As they should.

"I'm Happy and I'm fine"
Her spirit spoke to mine
"And the dinner you girls made—
Looked real good"

First Night at Boarding School

Age 5 Years Old

When I was just a little child
I heard a voice most plain
It filled my soul—I remember still
The comfort that it gave

"Be not afraid, I am with you"
Those words today remain—
The power of that message
Alleviating all the pain

Sweet words that I have drawn upon
Throughout these many years
A message straight from Heaven
Soothed a young girls' fears and tears

A child in kneeling said her Prayers
To a Father not long left—
She knew just who to turn to
When drowning in distress

Be not afraid, I am with you
The voice with compassion said
And love and understanding
Fell upon her troubled head

Chapter Four

Everything Else Random Will Be

Random Thoughts

Design your own life's Template
Create a pallet of beauty
Let your light shine.

An Abstract Impression—
As we cast design from essence
Inspiration flourishes
Like an anthem for Picasso

Observe structures Expose it
Imitate—imagine—reflect
Life is a canvas
With pen to create
Paint to decorate Clay to sculpt
And music to dream.

Behold! A collage of color
Pastel patterns beneath an azure sky—
Water lilies languish
Upon liquid shimmers—
Rose petal beauty Posing
As if A Monet garden.

A gorgeous sculpt
Is like a cut diamond—
Clay untouched
But a stone!

Appearances loom
Blinding the soul—
But an embracing heart
Opens the eyes.

Recall the storm
Embrace the calm—
Flee the clouds
But wonder at the rainbow.

Dream life,
Create beauty,
Build love.

Inspiration ignored
Is like clay—unsculpt'd
Inspiration acknowledged
Is a masterpiece in progress

Another's Birthday—typical
Your Birthday—Extraordinary

When anger simmers
Let Humor—boil!

May tragedy smooth your soul
And comedy etch your heart.

May your life mirror a classical ballet—
Exhibit discipline
Perform with grace
Create beauty
Strive for balance.

How surreal you are—
Like an abstract portrait
Angular—yet
Surprisingly symmetric.

The butterfly—flutters Petal to petal
And at this moment in time
My eyes only—behold her beauty.

Skinny on Thinny

So this is the skinny on Thinny?
Now I have a tale to tell...
About a Hunk...of Chocolate Chunk...
That the salesman is trying to sell!

Now Thinny was trying to gain some weight
To fill out her clothes you see...
She came to that man with hope in her voice...
Saying..."Please, you have to help me"

He gave her 10 servings of Chunk a Hunk
Double portions at that...if you please...
She then returned 80 days in a row...
Dragging herself on her knees...

At last Thinny Minny was no longer Skinny
Her clothes just no longer fit...
She dragged herself here...and dragged herself there
And finally could no longer sit.

She was lacking a lap, the chair was too small

Her knees blended into her chins

She had to remodel all of her clothes

For the seams were secured with pins!

Halloween Fright

Halloween night is the scariest night...
It fills me quite with fright!
Are you afraid when the nighttime shade
Blocks out the daytime light?

Of Ghosts and Goblins, Black Cats too...
I find myself most scared...are you?
Especially when they cross the street...
And Holler loud...TRICK OR TREAT!!!!

Computer Confusion

Ink...Ink...Just makes me think
These new inventions really stink!

Bring back the Smiths and the Brother
I'll peck the keys...I'd really Ruther...

Paper...Paper tons of Paper
I feel I'm involved...
In the "Great Paper Caper".

Printer, Printer...Summer thru winter
Runs so fast...this "Personal Sprinter"

Screen, Screen, I think I'll scream...
Another "POP UP"...is this a dream?

Keyboard, Keyboard...too many keys
Hand me the Telephone...
PLEASE PLEASE PLEASE

My brain and fingers
Are NUMB NUMB NUMB.
I'm in the fetal position...
Just sucking my thumb!!

This is you Lucky Day!

My dogs Lucas and Bobby
Limo and Pal...
Georgie and Jimbo
Delilah and Sal...

These are my Workers
They Help with the Mutts
They're willing to work
For not very much

They'll be all you want
They're for Hire you see
No Scratching or Barking
And not one Single Flea!

It's Fixed!

Yes, the Computer's back...
Just like you said...
And I am feeling Sassy...

E Mails are flying
Out of my head
I'm just a typing Lassie!

I thought twas my fault
That I was in error
Could that possibly be?

Oh well never worry
I'm just a terror
And it's working
As you can see.

Besides sending mail
I'll seek out a game
Solitaires usually the name...

Memory and Gigabytes
Servers and Spam
Now (Isn't that a name for ham?)

Yes the Computer's back
But so's the operator...
Cross your fingers and your toes
And (I hope) to write you later!

Inquire Within

What is it you wish?
What do you desire?
Have you considered this...?
"Have Mutt...just for Hire"

Will be all you want...
For 3 squares a day...
Will sit on your lap...
Catch vermin or Play!

Will be your Companion
Or Protector of sorts
Will "smile" or Roll Over
"Speak" or give "Snorts"

Or is it a Pedigree
You're hankerin' for
A Blue Blooded Bichon
(Somewhat of a Bore)

Are you a Walker...a Runner?
And need help to "Pace"
Are you seeking Protection...
So as not to use Mace?

Well, you've now hit the Jackpot
And I dear to Say...
Come into my Shoppe...

A Course in Horses

What you say about Dogs is true
And Cats can make you laugh...
Dogs have Masters...so they say
And Cats...well they have Staff!

Horses on the other hand
Are big and kinda scary...
Their Teeth are large, their Nostrils too
And their Necks and Tails are hairy!

Now I've been thrown more than once
I've found it less than fun...
But Prince Charles has too - so I can say
I'm not the only one!

As a Child I went to Riding School
In Jodhpurs and riding Boots
Dressage and Jumping was the norm
But that didn't help me...Toots!

My Friend Flicka was read to me
As a bedtime story each night...
And Trigger was a Hero...but
He wasn't in my sight!

But nothing really served me well
A Love of Horses...is not in force
All I can say...I'm sorry for this...
A Horse is a Horse
Of Course of Course!
A Horse is a Horse of Course!!

Doggie in the Window Pet Shop Blues

I'm SORRY to say
Reality Sucks...
I'm SORRY your dreams
Didn't pay Big Bucks

I'm SORRY depression
Has come your way...
I'm SORRY, I'm SORRY
Tis all I can say!

I'm SORRY the Masses
Didn't seek you out...
I'm SORRY reality's
All you've got!

I'm SORRY it's back
To The Window once more...
I'm SORRY no Buyers
Will come to the Store.

I'm SORRY to say...
One of a Kind doesn't cut it...
I'm SORRY to say you will
JUST HAVE TO MUTT IT!

Four Stanzas

You people ARE driving me crazy
All I can write is a rhyme
My thinking is also distorted
And I'm speaking in three quarter time!

It's one thing to share this with you too
But strangers just don't understand...
It takes me 4 stanzas to greet them
Another, to shake their hand!

So I will try to shorten this
Ornaments, finish, today...
Material, Wal-Mart, pattern, Slim fast
...that's all I can say!!

Living the "Good Life"

I am living the "Good Life"
Of this I am sure
I am not beaten down
And I plan to endure

This age I've arrived at
I am grateful to see
The wrinkles and gray hairs
Define who is me...

Of good times and bad
The good...far outweigh...
And I'm grateful for all...
I am given each day.

You must look at life
With a humorous eye...
But along with the laughter
An occasional cry!

Not for one's self
In a self-pitying way
But for others misfortunes and
Their darkest day.

I guess the best thing
You can do for another...
Is simply embrace them...
Brother to Brother...

WHAT I'VE LEARNED

You can't just be silly because you tell the world that you want to be silly. What is silly anyway? I think when we are old and act silly—people look at you funny.

GIVE UNTO OTHERS

In the early 1930's my young parents hosting a party answered a knock at the door. There stood a man asking for spare change for food. My father returning to the festivities and amid unwarranted negative comments and speculation as to how the donations should be used, collected the monies from his guests. At the end of the party all gathered on the porch to say their goodbyes. They were shocked to see stacked neatly in the corner—by one who overheated their unkindness directed at him—all the monies given earlier. Lesson—give unconditionally. If you do this unto the least of these, you do it unto me.

MAKE PEACE

At the start of each New Year, we have just a few short hours to make peace with our past, so it won't screw up our future. If we can right just one wrong before January 1st. then we might learn that love, not time, heals all wounds. Believe in miracles.

PERSPECTIVE

We should not compare our lives to others. We have no idea what their journey is all about. All that really matters in the end is that we loved.

COMPASSION

That unfortunately I have become desensitized to the murder and mayhem of the day—but—I cannot abide the suffering of any helpless animal at the hands of Human? Kind.

ANGELS UNAWARE

We should welcome all who come into our lives. It's been said that some come as Blessings others as lessons. Either way, I believe that we have the ability to entertain Angels. We should open our minds and hearts and dismiss no one—lest we pass—Angels unaware.

OLD AGE

This getting old isn't too bad. You can say what you want. Act as you wish. Kick in selective hearing and sore muscles and joints. Close your eyes as if resting, and basically do what you want. If you don't makes waves—ha ha.

FOR A WHILE

There are those in Life that just make you smile, laugh and live just a little bit better—For that I say—Thank You.

AUTUMN

Well, today is the First Day of Fall (my personal favorite). Our traditional scarecrows are standing at attention around the picket fence, nestled amongst the rose bushes, a contradiction of sorts, but that's California and that makes them happy! Their coats and hats are a bit worn, some have lost a bit of stuffing, leaving the others looking a bit overstuffed, but they stand tall with anticipation and big silly grins on their faces, longing for attention. I love all 13 of these wonderful, faithful friends, who demand nothing but a dab of glue, a bit of stuffing and an occasional new ribbon. You see, for me, they already have a brain, heart and courage, and I, thank goodness, have always been blessed with ruby red slippers—CLICK

BELLA

Remembering my 4 lb. Yorkie Bella. I often think of her. Such a sweet girl. I owned a gift store in Solvang, California called "Bella". One day my daughter Karen called to tell me that there was a little yorkie named "Bella" who needed a home. A match meant to be. We embarked on a journey tougher, that of a Pet Therapy Team, volunteering at a local hospital for a few years that was so rewarding. Most of the other dogs were big, wonderful and smart. Bella was the tiniest of them all. Able to cuddle up with her patients, all of them adults. She especially liked to visit the nurse's stations. One day while getting ready for our shift, I got ready to drive her in her pink scarf and ID badge. She looked at me and I knew she no longer had the enthusiasm for her "job". And on that day we retired. She gave all she could. Believe it or not, this is a very stressful calling, and the dogs are very sensitive to human suffering. She went on to live a carefree doggie life. I miss her. She had a Big Heart, for such a little peanut.

UNCLE DON

Planning to have another "Totally Awesome Day." So took a moment to reflect on Happy Thoughts. On that note, my happy thought is this—Having my uncle stand in the doorway, arm outstretched against the door jamb, and my 3 year old self swinging on his arm. All the more poignant—He was killed at age 19, Bataan Death March, 2nd. World War. Still, he gave me the awesome memory. A Happy Thought that has been with me these 84 years. Thank you Uncle Don.

TO MY 'MOTHERS'

To all you Mothers in my little corner of the world—Happy Mother's Day—I am so proud of all. Such beautiful women raising outstanding families with love, kindness and understanding. You are setting the bar high and teaching your children all the values they will need to live their lives successfully. As the matriarch in our family I thank you and love all—You are my Heart. XOXOXO

UPSTAIRS BEARS

This is the story
Of the Upstairs Bears
Who lived in a shop
At the top of the stairs
So many there were—
Twas hard to keep track
On tables, chairs, cupboards,
And benches they sat!

All colors and sizes—
Beribboned and plain
Some serious—silly—
Some sober, some sane
There was Teddy
Astride the big wooden horse
And General guarding the door of course—

Little Miss Molly—
Her eyes open wide
Keeping her eyes upon all inside
Jeffrey—Molasses, Big Brown Bear too—
And Samantha all decked out—minus a shoe

Yes, this is the story
Of the Upstairs Bears
Who lived in a shop
At the top of the stairs
Pouty Bear dressed up in a sweater of red
And Baby Bear Barney, snugly tucked into bed

Vickey with ribbons
Adorning each ear
And Black Bear and Melody
Sitting quietly near
Four furry friends in feathers and silk
Sit at the table, sharing cookies and milk

With fireplace blazing—
The room all aglow—
Sit warm cozy teddy bears—
Row after row
Yet their very fondest wish of all—
Is to be lovingly carried down the hall

Whether by arm—in a box or a sack
They really don't care—and that's a fact
They wait to be purchased at any price
By someone loving and special
And especially nice

A smile, a hug and a "You belong to me"
Is all they require from you—don't you see?
And in return believe it or not
You'll get the best friend you ever got

Yes, this is the story of the Upstairs Bears
Who lived in Solvang, at the top of the stairs
The shop they call home—yessiree
But only they hope—temporally

AUTUMN WITH AN "S"

"S" Stands for Scents

The smell of roasting turkey and pumpkin pie,
Cinnamon—spices—my oh my!
Cornbread dressing—beans, off the vine,
All these scents, are a very good sign.

The aroma of apples, straight from the tree,
Are ready for bobbing, for you and for me.
The scent of crisp air, gives a nip to my nose,
And I've added a sweater, giving warmth to my clothes.

The smell of a fire—which wood—I know not,
And mulled cider is fragrant—on the stove—in a pot,
Popcorn balls with molasses—oh so sweet,
Screams autumn to me—a harvest time treat!
"S" stands for senses, beautiful leaves—red, yellow and gold,
Are autumn's crown jewels—or so I've been told.
Orange and white pumpkins—from big to quite small,
Excite and entrance me—"it's autumn" they call.

Corn husks and scarecrows—my spirit just soars!
Standing by gates and decorating our doors.
Harvest corn—multicolored, and berries and nuts,
Are a feast for my senses, and touch them I must!

Bushel baskets of leaves and a rake standing near,
Tempts me to dump them, but, that's childish I fear.
A black crow, high above, is calling to me,
"It's autumn, awake, there's still much to see!"

"S" Stands for Scenes

The holiday kitchen—all pots, pans and lids,
Bustle with gramma, and moms and their kids.
The table arrayed with tradition, just sings,
With glass pilgrims and Indians, and thanksgiving things

There's tom turkey of clay, that my brother designed,
And small forest creatures, of every kind.
Autumn wreaths on the door, with green and gold bows,
And dining room chairs, set up, are in rows.

The table is large, for the grown and the vittles,
But a card table is needed to seat all the littles!
The family is growing—and what have we here,
One must sit at the breadboard? She's happy I fear!!

Ghost and goblins who come calling out, "trick or treat!"
And jack-o-lanterns make autumn, for me, quite complete,
Yes autumn with an "s"—scents, senses, and scenes;
Was made just for me, or at least, so it seems!

Seasons Never Faileth

What do you do in the Summertime
When all the World is Warm?
Do you Sail on the Sea, entice a Bee
Or Milk a Cow down on the Farm?

What do you do in the Autumn-time
When the Leaves are falling around?
Do you pick a Red Apple?
Drink Chilled Apple Snapple
Bundle Up in a Jacket of Down?

What do you do in the wintertime
When Jack Frost is nipping your Nose?
Do you Trim Christmas Trees,
Use a Hankie to Sneeze
Do you warm by the Fire...Your Toes?

What do you do in the Springtime
When all around you is New?
Do you marvel at Powers
Resulting in Flowers
That God has created for you?

Summertime, Autumn, Winter or Spring

Blustery, Freezing or Mild

I hope we give Thanks

For all that we have

And for being born...an American Child.

Patty Got A Peterbuilt

My Days are long and lonely
My Life is in a tilt
It's all because my honey's gone
And got a Peterbuilt

I've watched her get real restless
Her days at home were long
I guess I couldn't please her
Cuz now she's up and gone

Yes—Patty's got a Peterbuilt
A CB and a puppy—
She's on her way—All I can say
I hope that road ain't Bumpy

Oh she's racin' down the Highway
That gal that once was mine
Yes, Patty and her Peterbuilt
Are crossing County Lines

She plans to stop in Tulsa
Then on to Abilene
Yes, Patty's got a Peterbuilt
Every truckers dream

With stompin' Boots and Cowboy Hat
She sits and drives that team
The Horsepower pushes her down the road
That's one mean mighty machine

Yes, Patty's got a Peterbuilt
And when I saw her last—
She was racing down old 49
THAT GAL'S GOT LOTS OF CLASS!

Oh she's racin' down the Highway
That gal that once was mine
Yes, Patty and her Peterbuilt
Are crossing County Lines

Lessons

I think we are all like John Wilkes Booth
We choose to do OUR will...

We know instinctively right from wrong...
But make bad choices...still!

Why do you think that is the case?
Is it just the thrill of the act?

I think we like to push our luck...
Tempt fate...and that's a fact!

Sometimes we might be lucky...
Oftentimes we pay a price...

We should learn life's lessons early...
"Don't Run with Scissors" and "Play Nice"

Wasn't—Is

"I wonder what ever happened to..."
Have you ever said that phrase?
Have you wracked your brain, frustrated?
Sometimes for days and days?

I for one, have not...tis true...
Because??...This is my thought...
Cuz things I've lost...show up somehow
Whether I want them to or Not!

Take dust for an example...
I can lose it for a day...
Then turn around and there it is...
That's all that I can say!

How about those dandelions?
Pull them and they're gone...
VOILA...They're back...quick as a flash
As soon as you water the lawn!

An empty Gas tank...what a pain
You fill it...at great expense!!
Around the block a time or two
And it's empty or down to "cents"

Yes...things return in every way
So bother not, nor worry
Just take your time...like it or not...
It'll happen...so cease to hurry.

Like sending this Poem...an example...
I haven't written for days and days...
But we're back, myself and "Poem Girl"
What goes around just stays!!

So if any of this makes any sense
Or even if it doesn't...
I was gone...I'm back, for good or bad
I was...and then I wasn't!

But now I AM...for a while
I WERN'T I will try to be...not been...
I hope to stick around a Bit
I was out but now I'm IN...
Pat "wasn't—is"

Disasters California Style

Have you been reading the paper...
I should say...the weather reports?
Well here is California
They Predicted a Storm of sorts.

They warned of floods and mayhem
Due to the fires of late...
Without a 72 hour pack...
Sealed...would be our fate!

Mighty winds and angry surf
For days...we've been reminded...
The Weathermen foretold our doom
And then with relish...signed it!

Now, I for one was fearful
For those found in its path...
Mother Nature can be fierce...
And I cared not to feel her wrath!

But fear not, of course, as usual
The Weathermen cried wolf...
The rain, the wind and chaos
Served only to go "Poof"

And so I say, Predications...humpf...
And the Predictors of our fate...
You're only soothsayers after all...
Maligning our great State!

So now the sun is shining
No sprinkles are in store...
They're on to predicting earthquakes
With a rating of 8 or more...

California will fall into the ocean
Nevada will be the new Coast
Chasms miles wide we must manage
And plagues of all kinds we will host!

Yes, California has its own problems
Including reporters and such...
Don't forget the Weathermen
And all other Fruits and Nuts!

Rainy Daze

Today it's raining...think of that!
A surprise I must admit...
I heard the drops upon my roof
But didn't think of it...

I thought my sprinklers went awry
And sought to make a mess
So I just laid in sleepily haze
And went back to sleep I guess!

Upon awaking...what a shock
It's been at least a Year...
A single rain sound...fair I say...
Has touched my tender Ear.

I've found my Yellow Slicker
My Boots up to my Knee
The problem is...I wore them last
When I was only three!

So reality it Bites again...
Newspaper as a hat...
I grab the trash...and "Slipper Slush"
Now What Do You Think Of That?

Circus Trainer

I wondered how long it would take you
To go on to much better things...
I'm impressed...I really must tell you
Just think...The Star of Circus Three Rings!!

The Trapeze...now that is an answer
You've mastered the Goal—Crossbar...
 I'm sure you need little practice...
You've proven that you can fly far.

As a Clown, you would need little makeup
With THOSE eyes and toothless grin...
I know if you are but advertised
You're sure to pack them in!

Elephants, Tigers and Trampolines
Horses and Stilted Walkers
Dogs doing Tricks, The Sideshow too
Also the Carnival Hawkers!

If "Flying" isn't your cup of tea
I'm certain you'll find your niche...
You can always man the softball booth
And dispense those little Goldfish!

You'll always be my "Circus Star"
You won't be kicked around...
And I'll be very very sure
You won't go to the POUND.

I'll see you in the Circus...
Center Ring...You'll be the Star
And I will STAND and SALUTE you
HIP HIP HOORAY and HARDY HAR HAR!

Pitching Poetry

KETCHUP, Catch-up How very clever of you...
How bout PICKLE RELISH and...
A little MUSTARD too?

I'll PITCH a poem your way
You BUNT one back to me...
This way the SCORE is even...
We both are WINNERS...as you see.

It's all in how we PLAY this GAME
We both get up to BAT
I see us both as HITTERS
And that is simply that!

The FANS are going crazy...
Yet, one never hears a BOO
Of course the FANS consist of PROBABLY
—only...Me and You!

So help yourself to PEANUTS
POPCORN, SODA and/or BEER
MUSTARD, PICKLE RELISH, KETCHUP
FOOT-LONG HOTDOGS...it's all here

Keep PITCHING all that Poetry
No STRIKEOUTS, BALLS, this INNING
MY MITT is poised to CATCH it all...
And that's what we call WINNING.

Martyr Martyr

Martyr Martyr look at me
I'm a stinker, yessiree
Couldn't find a Protein Bar
After looking near and far...

Martyr Martyr Can it be
Corn and Taters I do see
Will that do? I declare
I also see some underwear!

Martyr Martyr...Oh my gosh
I thought I put them in the wash
But there they are upon the shelf
We'll self-suffice, so help yourself!

Martyr Martyr...We have it all
No Elves or Fairies in my "Mall"
But food and Undies you will find
Yet, NO PROTEIN BARS OF ANY KIND...

The Protein Blues

I've been checking the "Larder"
For a Protein Bar...
It's taken 2 days...
And no luck so far!

There is popcorn and beans
Potatoes and such...
But with a "bar" in your mind...
You don't want these that much.

I guess I'll try harder
In checking the "Larder"
Or maybe I'll barter
And just play the Martyr!

Nothing Better

Hola...Tacos, Enchilada and Beans
Rice, Rellenos, Tamales...it seems
I love them all...can't make a decision
Mexican Food is a Family Tradition!

I'm not from the South...of the Border and yet...
My taste in Food is the closest I get...
I own not a Serape, a Cacti or such...
But I Love a good Chili...Very Much.

I'll take a Burrito...Grande that is
No Margarita...but Coke with a Fizz...
Nachos will do...with a whole lot of cheese
Gracias Amigo...Please, Please, Please.

Passing Years

I'm afraid to visit the dentist...
I know that isn't proper...
But darn it all, it makes me mad
When He makes me that "fake chopper"

Then of course the Doctor
You look for TLC
All he says is takes this pill
It's age...go home and pee!

Now glasses...that's a different thing...
It's hard to read his signs...
But even worse ON glasses prescribed
To read twixt all the Lines!

I know we're supposed to exercise
But my Physical Vices are few...
I don't like Yoga, running or walking
There is NOTHING I plan to do!

So...there you are...Memory?
You must be kidding and so
With that in "Mind" (a Freudian Slip)
I give mine permission to go.

With all my other problems
I'm thinking "It's no big deal"
With no clothes, teeth, shoes or eyes
Need a Bargain? I'm a Steal

Stitches and Seams

A quilt is a positive thing
Many a thought it does bring...
Of stitches and seams...Faraway dreams...
And the colors just make your heart sing!

It reminds you of life in a way
Each piece has a lot it could say...
Of course it can't talk, sing, skip or walk
But it surely can brighten your day!

It would be great if a seam could mend
All that seems Problematic in each of our lives
Just think how the colors...Blending with others
Would smooth our poor tired eyes!

Yes, a quilt is a marvelous invention
To make one takes lots of attention
Just like waking each day...
Being nice I would say...
Makes life's really worthy to mention

So keep up the good work...
Make sure you don't shirk...
You might be stitching your life...
One never knows...how or why it all goes
But at least you'll be warm through the strife...

Karma

I guess the thing we need to remember...
Is what goes around...returns...

Kindness begets Kindness...
A Lesson we hope one learns!

The Golden Rule...so simple
Yet Beautiful in...Fact

In such poetic simplicity...
One can learn just how to Act.

I also love the Beatitudes...
They also guide the Way...

And all that's Written for our Good
If we'd just read and pray...

Love to Chat

I am the chat queen after all
At least that's what they say...
I only chat...just think of that...
When my computer has its day!

Sometimes it's up...sometimes it's down
Right now...straight as an arrow
The darn thing works...such perks...
I'm on the straight-n-narrow.

So what's with you...your words are few
It's me doin' all the chattin'
I'll read them all...those words of yours
In English, French or Latin!

Yes, I'm the chat queen...whoop tee do...
My words are bottled up...
I haven't vented for a while...
I've fillith up my cup...

So I'll keep on chattin'...spillin'
Out the words that tumble round...
They won't stay in...they're jumpin' out
Though I don't make a sound!

Goodbye from the queen of everything

Goodbye from this and that...

Goodbye from my realm of queendom

Goodbye from the queen of chat...and that's that...

George the Entertainer

George, George swinging from the Trees
Looking for Christmas...if you please!

I want to join your Jungle Chorus
May I be Lily the Treetop Loris?

We all can Jingle in the Jungle...
And try to outrun the Jungle Fungle...

George, George Look out for that Tree
Just keep entertaining little old me...

Young at Heart

May you never be too grown up
To search the skies on Christmas Eve
Hunt for colored eggs
Or look for Fairy Dust

Red, White and Blue

Today is Independence Day, even though it feels like so many of our Freedoms are being taken away on a daily basis. I want to remember that this is a blessed Land. I want to contemplate the words to the "Star Spangled Banner", "America The Beautiful", and "God Bless America". I want to honor the "Pledge Of Allegiance". I want to march to "Yankee Doodle" and "When Johnny Comes Marching Home" and immerse my being into the "Battle Hymn Of The Republic" sung by the Mormon Tabernacle Choir. This is what American is to me. "God Bless America", I will celebrate today this National Holiday—But—I will remember and be grateful for this beautiful Country. "This Land Is Your Land"—this Land is My Land—Remember Her—Appreciate Her—Care for Her, and—Pray for Her.

Gratitude

Sometimes we just need to look up,
Smile and say
I know that was You—
Thank you!

Good Advice

I've learned from Experience— Please Heed—
If you are having A Bad Day—
DO NOT CUT YOUR BANGS

Chapter Five

An Exercise in ABCs

To You Who May Be Reading This
I've Got A Lot to Say
I Will Start By Sharing My ABCs
In A Most Unusual Way

My Typist Cheryl Calls It Prose
She's Right On—I Suppose
So it's ABC—Right Down To Z
My Poetically Promising Prose

A

To Whom It May Concern
I'm aspiring to Activate
An Activity Anew
Going thru the Alphabet
Albeit annoying to you

I Always Admire
Anything I find a bit askew
I hope you will Appreciate
My efforts—now Adieu

B

Bye Bye of course
Is the same as adieu
TaTa, adios or
Good riddance to you!

Bye Bye Blackbird
Bye Bye Baby
Bon voyage
See you later...maybe...

Yes..."B" is for Bye Bye
Bye Bye Blues...
I'll write you later...
With all my "C" news!

C

Today's lesson as you will see...
Will be finding a word
Beginning with "C"

A popular word for C is Cat
But I'm not really thrilled with that...
Calico just came to mind
A Cat of Course of a Colorful kind.

I vowed no poems concerning a Cat
But Creepin' Critter, I'm doin' just that!

It's Clear I'm Calm
In my Circle of Choices
But Circumstances Call
Only Cat voices...

Cats are cleverly
Leaving their Clues...
Their Complicating
And corrupting views!

I'll no longer Compile or Compose
This poem For Cats,
I Confess, might Cause me
To Conform.

D

We've been through
A and B and C
So now it's time
To feature "D"

I plan to Develop
A Deviate Doll...
A Dull, Dumb Doofus...
For a Desert Mall!

I'll duplicate
This Dizzy Dummy

With Double vision
And Doughnut shaped tummy

He'll be Downtrodden,
Dull witted and drab
A Dressmakers Dream
To Design for rehab

But I'm only a Dreamer...
(My Definite Downfall)
My "Deviate Doll"
Is a Drummed up "Doubtful"

E

I'm here in the East...
Entertainingly merry
Eating Edibles Entirely
...made up of dairy.

Enthused and enticed
By such an Event
Such an Evening, 'tis Evident,
I've never spent.

I'll Explain and Expose
Exactly my plight...
I'm Essentially Evading
The dawns early light.

Escargot and Eggplant
Are not on my menu...
Europe Especially,
Is not part of my venue.

The Essence of Edibles
In my Estimation...
Is nothing more,
Than Eggs-a-gyration!

F

There was a Fraternity
Of Fortunate Fellows...
Fully grown, friendly,
From Pocatello

Fancy of Feet...
Frivolous too...

With a Fondness
Of finding things to do...

Flippant and Foolish...
Flagrantly Frank...
A Formula Forcing
Many a prank!

Frightfully Fickle...
Frequently Faint
This Fellowship Follower's
Formal...he ain't!

Full of Frame...
With Freckled nose
A Foolish sight
In Flowered clothes...

A Fashion Failure...
'Tis no lie...
He wore a Fuchsia
In his Fly!

G

A Gaudy General...
In Galoshes...did gamble
Galloping...Gallantly...
Through thicket and bramble

He gambled all Games...
Gathering Gems and Gear
Genuine Garbage
And Germanic beer

A Glutton with Gloves
Guarding Gnarled hands
In Glory or Gloom
He governed his lands

He Gradually Greeted
The reaper most Grim
This Gambler lost...
'Twas the end of Him!

H

Harold Stevens Hopper...
Hopscotched to Hana
Honestly Hoping to
Harvest some manna...

With a Hat on His Head...
He Harmoniously Hummed
And He Hastened and Hied...
Happy not dumb!

Handsome and Hardy...
Hawaii He Haunted...
Head over Heels...
On to Hana He sauntered...

He was Headstrong and Healthy...
But hungry of sorts
If Hana was Heaven...
Then Harold Stevens Had warts!

Harold Hopper...Heartbroken...
Hopelessly fled...

No Hana...no manna...
No Harvest...He said...

Hello...to His Homeland...
Happy...unharmed...
And sang for His supper...
So be not alarmed!!

I

Ivan the Ignorant...
Impeached by the Imp
Incoherently Indifferent...
Walked with a limp!

Injustice he cried...
Indiscreetly...Inflamed
Ivan the Ignorant
Is what I've been named!

You've insulted my Ignorance
Impeaching me so...
Intolerant In regard to my Limp...
As you know.

You've indirectly
Induced the Impulse to flee
But your Improper Ideas
Have imprisoned me!

Ivan the Ignorant
With Imbalance...Imbibed...
Indigestion followed...
No Illness Implied.

Ivan the Ignorant...
Impeached by the Imp
Ill-mannered and Impudent...

Still walked with a Limp!

J

Do Judges Justify Justly?
Do Judges Judge with fury?
Do Judges Joke on Judgement day?
Do Judges Judge Judges and Jury?

Do Judges act as court Jesters?

Do Judges Jail court pesterers?

Do Judges Journey to the "Joint"?

Do Judges Jump to make a point?

Do Judges Judge John Doe?

Do Judges Jam with Jazzers?

Do Judges Judge the Joyless?

Are Judges Razmatazzers?

K

Kettles of Ketchup

Were Kept by the King

Among with Knickknacks

A Knife and some string...

Kindhearted and Klunky

A Kindly old man

He Kicked up the Kindling...

As he sat by his fan.

His Kingdom was King sized...

With Kin all about...

The Keeper of Kettles...
Was Knobby and stout.

With Kittens and Kites
He kicked off the day
Calling all Kids...
In the Kitchen they'd play.

L

Lines of Laundry
Loftily blew.
Looming Loosely...
Leisurely...too!

Lightning Lavished
With Lawlessness

Labored Locally...
What a mess!

Rain Loudly Loitered...
And the Laundry Line...
Was Limp with Linen...

Now...not so fine...
Literally Loaded...
Lopsided and Low...
Rain soaked Laundry...
Has a Long way to go...

Logically speaking...
The Laundry was Lost
The Liquid Literally...
Leveled much cost...

So Look to the Lightning
Still Lingering above
And Long for clean Linens
And a DRYER to Love!!!!!

M

The Magician Magnificent...
Said to the Maid
"Make believe...not Magic...
Make Merry...be staid.

Manage your Manners...
For there are Many
Matter of fact...
Manage each penny!
Be Mentally Merciful...
Not Messy but Mild
Mightily Moderate...
Moral not wild!

Don't Mutilate Music
With Mundane notes
Don't muddle poetry
With Mindless quotes!

Marry a Millionaire...
With Minimum faults
Not a Miserable Miser...
Worth not his salts!

Don't Mislead, Mismanage
And don't misguide
Be a Model Mistress
Not given to pride.

And Magic Moments
Shall Monopolize"
Said the Magician Magnificent...
With Mysterious eyes.

N

The Native was Naked
Without a Name
A Noiseless Nomad...
Numbed with pain...

No way Nurtured...
Needing a Nurse...
Lacking Nutrition...
A Noticeable curse!

Yet nobly he did
Nod my way...
Nonsensically speaking...
This he did say...

"Newcomer, Nightmare,
Nimble and News

Nonchalant, Nickel,
Needle, (some clues)?

As a Naturalist...
I Naturally Noted
This Native Neglected
(Nor never quoted...)

His Neighbors, his Nation,
The ring in his Nose
His Nonviolent Nature...
Non-existent clothes.

Nonetheless, I've indeed
Nurtured a Notion...
(Notwithstanding
He lives across the ocean...)

The Narrative the Native
Needed to say
Were words on a Newspaper
He found one day...

Never mind the fact...
He didn't understand...
Nonetheless...he spoke...
To this Nonresident man!

O

The Operators Opinion...
Offended poor Otto...
She had obviously lost
The Odds on Lotto...

Oddly Off balance...
Otto openly swore...
Opposing her attitude...
He walked out the door!

He felt her Outrageous...
An Outlaw at best...
An Oddball poor loser...
The Optimum pest...

"Organized gambling...
Outweighs any fun"

This overrated Operator...
Had not won!!

Otto...Overheated...
And just overworked...
Outwardly Outraged...
Acted the jerk!

It was time to Omit
Such Offensive Ongoing...
He opened his mind...
To oppose tantrum throwing...

Otto and "Olga"
To dinner they went...
Ordering Olives and Oranges...
A nice time was spent!

P

Please Pass the Potatoes,
The Peas and Pork
Party guests are Prepared
With knife and fork!

Each Person is pleasantly
Poised to take Part...
Passing with Passion...
Each Plate...with glad heart!

The Patios Pretty
With Pansies...Pale Pink...
All Plantings Prepared
In the Potting shed sink.

With Piano Playing
And Platters Piled high
The Prayer has been said...
We proceed with a sigh...

Professionals serve
With such prominent air...
The Program Progresses...
Providing the fare...

The Produce is fresh...
I'm Profoundly at Peace...
The Planning panned out...
My worries can cease!

Just bring on the Pastry...

Puddings and cakes...

Perhaps...these (and Presents)

...a Party makes!!!!

Q

The Qualifications

Of Quilting a Quilt...

Have no Qualms...

Hands free of silt!

Use quaint fabrics...

Quadrangle each piece...

Quarters will do...

Question each crease!

Work Quickly and Quietly

With nary a Quirk

Do not quit my dear

Nor Quilting shirk!

The Queen of Quilting...

That is you...

Quite the "Bee"
In all you do!!

R

Repeal and Repent
Repair and Repay
Be Reluctant to Render
Resentment this day

Respect and Respond
But do not reverse
Or you will incur
A Regrettable curse

S

The Silly old Scarecrow
Was Slumped on a Stick
Short in Stature
And dressed like a hick

Stuck in the Soil
He suffered a lot

Stubbornly hailing
To Show what he's got

Shoo away Sparrows
Do Something Super
But the Silly old Scarecrow
Still stands in a Stupor

T

The Tattooed man
In Tap shoes danced
And played his Tambourine

He tapped as fast as he could
Tap and all the folks said,
"Look at That!"
The Tattooed man - Just Tapped Today
Twenty Times better than yesterday

U

"Unpen the Unicorn" he pled
"Unfix the Unfit gate"

Uncle Urged and Uttered
"Before it grows too late!"

V

Vicky Vee had Violet eyes
Her Vision was Very amazing
Voicing colors...Vanishing dull
Her Violet eyes were blazing

W

Webster Went to Washington
Riding With his Watchman
Whither here or whither there
They Wander When and
Where they can

"Webster," said the Watchman
"Where Will We Wander...do you care?"
Webster answered, "This I know...
"We'll just Wander till We get there"...

X

X-ray Xtra Xample Xcellent
Try all three
Xylophone another X
I'm Xtremely Xcited you see

Y

Try Yelling said I
You'll feel better
A Yodel will bring
You much joy

Yankee Doodle Your way
Is all I can say
To brighten your day
Young boy

Z

Zebra played the Zylaphone
Zen like friends approved
Zebra Zapped the Zylo keys
And nary a person moved

Now I've finished The ABCs
Give Me Applause—If You Please
So Happy "Numbers" I Cannot Bring
Cuz Math Definitely Is Not My Thing—

ABOUT THE AUTHOR

Patricia Ann Hopper was born in 1936 in New York City to talented and creative parents. Their gifts were not lost on their daughter who inherited qualities she would enjoy and exhibit all throughout her life. Creative writing, decorating, music and art, plus love of family fill her days. She married her high school love, Paul Berney. Together, they have enjoyed an active, successful and satisfying life. They have 5 children and many grandchildren and great-grandchildren.

ACKNOWLEDGEMENTS

Thank you to my dearest Paul and my angel daughter Cheryl for the BIG part you played in this 'production.' Paul, my biggest cheerleader and to Cheryl my 'Tilly the Typist.' To Scott, the cover is dedicated to you. Also, love to any and all who have expressed interest in my 'doings.'

A special thank you to Greg Marshall who, without his talents and efforts, this 'work of art' would have remained on the shelf. If it takes a village to raise a child, then it takes a husband, daughter and friend to raise an 'authoress'.

www.ingramcontent.com/pod-product-compliance
Lightning Source LLC
Chambersburg PA
CBHW080947050426

42337CB00055B/4580